Just Living by Faith

A Study Guide to Habakkuk in the 20th Century

Andrew T. LePeau
Phyllis J. LePeau
John D. Stewart

InterVarsity Press
Downers Grove
Illinois 60515

© 1979 by Inter-Varsity Christian
Fellowship of the United States of America

All rights reserved. No part of this book
may be reproduced in any form without
written permission from InterVarsity Press.

InterVarsity Press is the book-publishing
division of Inter-Varsity Christian
Fellowship, a student movement active on
campus at hundreds of universities, colleges
and schools of nursing. For information
about local and regional activities, write
IVCF, 233 Langdon St., Madison, WI 53703.

Distributed in Canada through
InterVarsity Press, 1875 Leslie St., Unit 10,
Don Mills, Ontario M3B 2M5, Canada.

ISBN 0-87784-586-7

Printed in the United States of America

239

Introduction

Even in people there is often something which resembles
changelessness. At a class reunion we might say, "Good ol'
George! He hasn't changed a bit!" when George pulls a stunt
such as he was known for years ago in school. It is the far
more dependable changelessness of God which Habakkuk
celebrated when he exclaimed, "His ways were as of old"
(Hab. 3:6), or as we might say, "He hasn't changed a bit!"
The details of his working change with each age and situation, but you can rely on his faithfulness, his wrath toward
wickedness and injustice, his compassion toward humility
and obedience.

God's faithfulness is the basis for Habakkuk's confidence
that "the righteous shall live by his faith" (Hab. 2:4). But this
was a difficult conclusion to reach. Faced with injustice in his
own country and the physical violence it provoked, faced
further with the militarism of Babylon which threatened to
(and finally did) sweep over Judah, faced, in short, with the
apparent success of wickedness on personal, national and
international levels, Habakkuk asked, "What is the point of
continuing to be faithful? What advantage is there in obeying
God's law? Since everyone is living and succeeding by wickedness, how are the righteous to live at all?"

Habakkuk agonized over these questions. And the questions remain today. Why is there so much evil in the world,
and why do we seem helpless to do anything about it? Why
are some people living in luxury while others toil only to be
robbed? How can laws originally intended to insure justice

for the helpless end up filling the pockets of the greedy? Why do countries which supposedly stand for freedom and justice support other countries which explicitly or implicitly do not? Because such questions are being asked so forcibly and insistently today, the message of Habakkuk and his fellow minor prophets are being rediscovered. More than perhaps any other Old Testament writer, Habakkuk reveals his inner struggle to have faith and live righteously in the face of the apparent futility of faithfulness.

Despite the apparent rise of evil all around and despite the increased awareness among Christians toward doing something about it, the rediscovery of the minor prophets has been all too slow. The lure of the familiar has too often won out. Our goal in this guide is to open up the book of Habakkuk to study. More specifically, the purposes are: to identify with Habakkuk's questioning of God; to understand God's attitude toward evil; to see how the character of evil as given in Habakkuk has parallels in our world today; and to learn to respond to God and to evil as the righteous who live by faith, not as the wicked who trust in themselves. It is also our intent that those who use this guide will come to understand the view of history expressed in Habakkuk and begin to see how our view of history determines our attitude and response to wickedness.

One of the difficulties in studying Habakkuk is that so little of the historical setting is given. Habakkuk assumes we already know it. The people the book was originally written for did. We must look elsewhere, however, for this essential information. For this reason, after an initial overview of Habakkuk, the second study examines 2 Chronicles 33—36 which gives the historical background of Habakkuk's time. Of the remaining studies, the third through the sixth focus in turn on four major divisions of Habakkuk. The seventh helps put it all together.

This guide follows the text of the Revised Standard Version of the Bible. Though it is not necessary to use this version, it may be helpful. If the study is used in a group, it is especially helpful to have everyone use the same translation. In general, a modern translation is recommended rather than a paraphrase or an older, archaic version. In a group setting, each member may also wish to have a copy of the study guide to record observations before the group meeting and then to note the insights of others. The group leader should also read the notes in the back of the guide before the study. These give some hints on how to get the most out of a group discussion.

We can count on God and his promises. He promised his Spirit would help us understand and live out his Word. We can rely on it.

Study 1
A First Look

Habakkuk 1–3

Purposes
☐ To see the structure of the book of Habakkuk.
☐ To understand Habakkuk's attitude toward evil and your own.
☐ To see how Habakkuk's attitude changes in the course of the book.

If God is all-good and all-powerful, so goes the argument, how can he allow evil to exist? This is not a uniquely modern challenge to the Judeo-Christian faith. Job struggled with it. So did the prophet Habakkuk.

Very little is known about Habakkuk himself. He probably lived in Judah around the late seventh to early sixth century B.C. This was about four hundred years after David and just prior to the Babylonian exile. Thus he was a contemporary of the prophet Jeremiah.

Notes on the Text
1:1 *prophet*—except for Haggai, this is the only instance in which such a designation is used in the first sentence of an Old Testament book. This may mean that Habakkuk held this position as an official public office.

3:1 *Shigionoth*—a musical instruction of uncertain meaning; therefore it is transliterated. Possibly it means this prayer is to be sung with great emotion.

3:19 *with stringed instruments*—a musical direction given to the leader of the temple's music, indicating that this prayer, and possibly the whole book, was to be used in public worship.

1. How do you respond to injustice in the world? in the Christian community? in your own life?

_____

_____

_____

_____

2. Read the book of Habakkuk. Who are the speakers?

_____

What are the major divisions of the book?

_____

_____

_____

3. What is Habakkuk's initial complaint?

_____

_____

_____

How is Judah described (1:2-4)?

_____

_____

How does God respond to Habakkuk's initial complaint (1:5-11)?

_____

_____

What effect does God's response have on Habakkuk (1: 12-17)?

_____

_____

What does he argue back?

_____

_____

How do you identify with the prophet's questioning?

_____

_____

4. In 2:1 what does Habakkuk finally do?

_____

How else could Habakkuk have responded to God?

_____

_____

5. What elements of true dialog are evident in the exchanges between God and Habakkuk up to this point?

_____

_____

_____

6. Against whom are the five woes (2:6-20)? Summarize each one.

_____

_____

_____

_____

What are some similarities among the five woes?

_____

_____

7. What does Habakkuk request from God in 3:2?

_____

What works of God are described in chapter 3?

_____

_____

_____

How is the mercy of God described in chapter 3?

_____

8. What attitudes and characteristics does Habakkuk demonstrate throughout the book?

_____

_____

9. How is the character of God demonstrated?

What characteristics of God are revealed?

10. What changes have occurred in Habakkuk through dialog with God?

11. Having seen the character of God in the book of Habakkuk, how has your attitude toward evil changed?

Study 2
Habakkuk in Perspective

2 Chronicles 33–36

Purposes
☐ To understand the historical context of Habakkuk.
☐ To see that as God dealt with nations in Habakkuk's time, so he does today; and to see on what grounds he acts.
☐ To see the fulfillment of Habakkuk's prophecy.

People often find the minor prophets difficult to understand. As we said in the introduction, this is so partly because these prophecies are generally addressed to specific historical situations usually without giving information about them except by inference. 2 Chronicles 33—36 (and 2 Kings 21—25) contain the historical account of the period immediately surrounding Habakkuk's prophecy. Though Assyria had been the dominant power in the Middle East, Nebuchadnezzar and the Chaldeans (another name for the Babylonians) were on the rise but had not yet invaded Jerusalem when Habakkuk brought his case before the Lord. Read these chapters in 2 Chronicles now, watching primarily for the basic history of the period.

Notes on the Text
33:3; *Baals*—the Hebrew *ba'al* means "master" or "posses-
34:4   sor." Since each piece of land had its own deity or
       owner, the Israelites found many Baals when they en-
       tered Canaan. Baal worship challenged the wor-ship
       of Yahweh throughout Israelite history. (See *The New
       Bible Dictionary,* p. 115.)
       Asherah [pl., *Asherim*]—a Canaanite mother-goddess.
       (See *The New Bible Dictionary,* p. 95, as well as

2 Chron. 33:19; 34:3-4, 7.)

33:6   *valley of the son of Hinnom*—a valley south of Jerusalem associated at this time with Molech worship, an important part of which was child sacrifice. Josiah's reforms put an end to this.

33:14   *outer wall*—built for the city's protection; Gihon is a spring, east of Jerusalem in the Kidron Valley, which helped supply the city's water needs; Ophel apparently referred to the southeast hill of the city; the Fish Gate was located at the north central part of the wall.

35:3   *holy ark*—an elaborately adorned box containing the two tablets of the Ten Commandments, some manna from the years of wandering in the desert and Aaron's rod (Ex. 25:10-22; Heb. 9:4-5). It served as a sign of God's presence. (See *The New Bible Dictionary,* p. 82.)

35:20   *Carchemish*—a city north and east of Israel on the Euphrates. As the Assyrian Empire began to crumble (612-609 B.C.), her Egyptian ally under Pharaoh Neco laid claim to Palestine and ordered it to pay tribute. Not long afterward, in 605 B.C., the Babylonians under Nebuchadnezzar II routed the Egyptian forces at Carchemish leading to the eventual Babylonian takeover of Palestine.

35:25   *Jeremiah*—the prophet; his lament mentioned here has not been preserved.

36:21   *seventy years*—Jeremiah predicted that Judah would be enslaved by Babylon for seventy years (Jer. 25:11-12; 29:10). The Chronicler comments that the land kept seventy sabbath years of rest to make up for the many years Judah had failed to keep the land fallow under the rule of her evil kings. (See Ex. 23:10-11 and Lev. 26:27-35.)

36:22   *Cyrus*—King of Persia who conquered Babylon, entering the capital itself in 539 B.C.

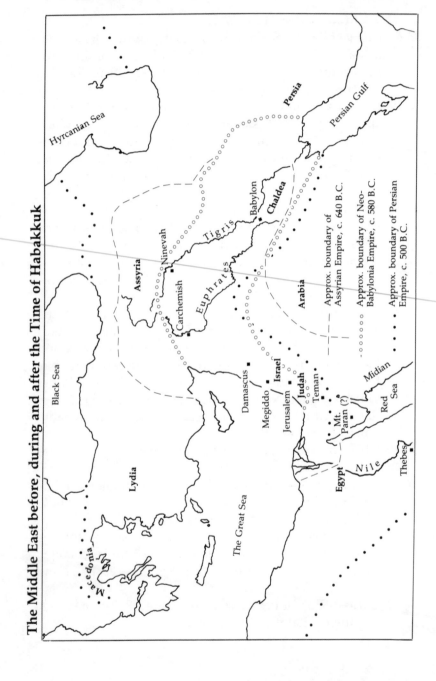

The Middle East before, during and after the Time of Habakkuk

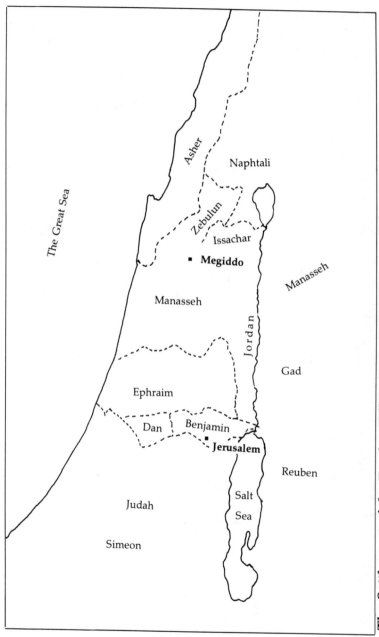

Asher

Naphtali

The Great Sea

Zebulun

Issachar

■ **Megiddo**

Manasseh

Manasseh

Jordan

Ephraim

Gad

Dan

Benjamin

■ **Jerusalem**

Reuben

Salt
Sea

Judah

Simeon

The Settlement of the Twelve Tribes in the Promised Land

Time Chart of Events during 2 Chronicles 33—36*

722 B.C. ————Samaria captured by Shalmaneser V of Assyria.

695 ————Manasseh begins his reign (33:1).

641 ————Manasseh dies; Amon begins his reign (33:20-21).

639 ————Amon assassinated; Josiah made king (33:24-25).

631 ————Josiah's reformation begins (34:2-3).

621 ————the law scroll discovered (34:8, 14).

612 ————Ninevah, capital of the Assyrian Empire, falls.

609 ————Josiah dies in battle of Megiddo (35:20-24); Jehoahaz crowned, then deposed after three months and taken to Egypt by Neco; Eliakim (Jehoiakim) crowned by Neco (36:1-4).

605 ————battle of Carchemish.

597 ————Jerusalem taken; Jehoiakim captured (36:5-6); Jehoiachin reigns three months and ten days; Zedekiah crowned by Nebuchadnezzar (36:9-10).

587 ————destruction of Jerusalem; Zedekiah taken captive by Nebuchadnezzar (36:17-21).

539 ————Babylon captured by Cyrus II, king of Persia (see 36:22-23).

Assyrian Empire

Babylonian (Chaldean) Empire

Persian Empire

Scholars continue to debate these dates, but they are approximately correct.

1. What kings are mentioned in 2 Chronicles 33—36? What kinds of information are given for each king?

_____

_____

_____

_____

2. What nations are mentioned (for example, in 33:11; 35:20—36:23)?

_____

In 36:2-4 what nation dominates?

_____

In 36:6-21 who wields power in Palestine?

_____

What does that say of the relationship between Babylon and Egypt?

_____

What relationship does the Chronicler perceive between these nations and God (compare 33:9-13; 35:20-24; 36:17, 22-23)?

_____

_____

3. What seems to have been the normal spiritual state of the kings, priests and people of Judah during this time?

_____

How do each of the kings of Judah at this time respond to God's Word?

_____

_____

According to the Chronicler, what relationship exists between this spiritual condition and the treatment Judah receives from her neighbors?

_____

_____

For what purpose does God use the nations? (How, for example, was Manasseh humbled as seen in 33:10-13?)

_____

_____

4. How did Josiah first respond to the words of the Lord (34: 19—35:19)?

_____

Why was Josiah so surprised and dismayed when the law was read?

_____

5. What prophets are mentioned in 2 Chronicles 33—36?

_____

What role did they play?

_____

How were they regarded?

6. To see why it was important to let the "land enjoy its sabbaths" (36:21), look up Exodus 23:10-11. What is the principal reason given for letting the land rest every seventh year?

What might the violation of the sabbath year indicate about the people's treatment of the poor in general?

How might these conditions relate to Habakkuk's complaint (1:1-4) and the woes of Habakkuk 2?

7. How is your country insensitive to the poor?

How are you involved in or how do you participate in these wrongs?

_____

_____

_____

For Further Study
1. Read Exodus 31:12-17 for a better understanding of how keeping the sabbath was a sign of God's covenant with Israel.

Study 3
The Dialog Begins

Habakkuk 1:1-11

Purposes
☐ To see the parallels between Judah and Babylon.
☐ To see how the wickedness of Judah and Babylon (injustice and militarism) correspond to our world today.
☐ To understand the relationship between violence and idolatry (self-worship).

Much of the Bible concerns how God deals with individuals. At least as much, if not more, concerns how he deals with groups—with religious groups, with economic groups, with political groups. In this study we will see some of God's dealings with nations.

Notes on the Text
1:1 *oracle*—can also be translated "burden," being derived from the Hebrew word meaning "to lift up."
1:6 *Chaldeans*—the inhabitants of Mesopotamia who at this time made up the last Babylonian Empire.
1:9 *terror . . . goes before them*—the Hebrew is uncertain; can also be translated, as the Jerusalem Bible does, "their faces scorching like an east wind."
1:10 *heap up earth*—a technique for seizing a fortress or city; an enemy piles dirt against a wall and uses this earthen ramp to scale it.

1. Read Habakkuk 1:1-4. Who is Habakkuk speaking about to God?

2. How does Habakkuk describe the Judah of his time in these verses?

3. What does he mean by "the law is slacked" (v. 4)?

4. What is Habakkuk's heartfelt concern?

How would you summarize his complaint to God?

5. What indication is there that he had prayed for a long time with no apparent answer from God?

6. Do you think the prophet is showing doubt or faith or both in these verses? Explain.

7. Imagine yourself as a Judean hearing this prophecy. What is your response thus far?

What if you heard such a prophecy today against your own country?

8. Read Habakkuk 1:5-11. How does God describe the Chaldeans? How do they conduct their warfare?

9. What words found in verses 1-4 are repeated in this paragraph?

What is the significance of this?

10. Compare verse 7 with verses 10-11. Why is violence the logical outcome of the Chaldeans' "god"?

11. How does the evil of the Chaldeans and Judeans compare with evil today?

_____

_____

How does the Chaldean god compare with the gods of today?

_____

12. In what ways is this section a response to Habakkuk's complaint?

_____

_____

_____

13. Why does God say, "You would not believe if told"?

_____

Do you believe God would do (or is already doing) something like this today? Why or why not? (For example, what might God be teaching Christians by the spread of Communism in the world?)

_____

_____

_____

Study 4
The Dialog Continues

Habakkuk 1:12–2:5

Purposes
☐ To understand the new problem raised by Habakkuk's second exchange with God.
☐ To investigate the ways Habakkuk relates to God and God to Habakkuk.
☐ To understand how God's answer to Habakkuk is given here in a nutshell.

Violence. We hear about it so much on the news, we read about it so much in the papers, we see it so much on the screen that we have become insensitive, calloused. Of course we may be shocked at some particularly horrible act. But only then might we be led to ask why. Why do people do violence to other people? Robberies. Wars. Riots. Assaults. Prejudices. Why?

Essentially, violence requires a low view of another human being. If we truly considered others to have dignity and value by virtue of being made in God's image, violence would end. But if we can treat others like animals or like machines, like things less valuable than ourselves, then the seeds of violence have been planted.

Knowing these things, Habakkuk wonders how God can use a people notorious for violence to do his will. Is this really the kind of God he is? Habakkuk wants some answers.

Notes on the Text
1:12 *We shall not die*—a possible reference to God's covenant with the patriarchs. (Compare Gen. 17:1-8 and Ex. 32:7-14.)

1:16 *seine*—a large fishing net with floats at the top and weights at the bottom.

2:1 *tower*—possibly a literal tower the prophet used for private meditation.

what I will answer concerning my complaint—the New American Standard Bible gives an alternate reading: "how I may reply when I am reproved."

2:2 *he may run who reads it*—a Hebrew idiom with the sense that those who read the vision should be able to understand it clearly (even as they run by it, or so that they may run and do it or tell others about it).

2:4 *live by his faith*—the notion of faithfulness is also included in this phrase, not just holding certain beliefs.

2:5 *wine*—perhaps symbolic of a greedy, self-indulgent lifestyle. (Compare Deut. 32:32-33.)

Sheol—the word used in the Old Testament for the abode of the dead, here personified.

1. How would you describe a just judge?

2. Read 1:12-17. How does Habakkuk begin his second address to God? How is God described?

Why is it significant that Habakkuk begins his second complaint with such a description?

3. What other facts are stated in verses 12-13?

_____

What apparent inconsistencies does he observe?

_____

4. What or who makes men like the fish of the sea? That is, who is the *thou* spoken of in verse 14?

_____

Who is the *he* referred to in verses 15-17? What evidence supports your answer?

_____

5. To what is the net analogous? How does the net illustration emphasize Habakkuk's complaint?

_____

6. What similarities are there between Judah (1:3-4) and the Chaldeans (1:13-14)?

_____

7. When have you felt like Habakkuk, aware of injustice and frustrated? Describe situations today where the wicked are swallowing up those more righteous.

_____

_____

_____

8. Read 2:1-5. What is the significance of Habakkuk's taking his stand to watch?

_____

What does this demonstrate about how Habakkuk and God relate to each other?

_____

9. What does God begin to say to Habakkuk in verses 2-5?

_____

What is Habakkuk supposed to do with the vision?

_____

What is said about it?

_____

What is the vision?

_____

_____

10. What is the contrast in verse 4?

_____

What is faith?

_____

If you were Habakkuk, would you be satisfied with God's answer? Why or why not?

_____

How are "waiting" and "living by faith" similar?

11. In 2:5 the arrogant man is likened to Sheol and death. In particular, how is this true?

How, then, does this godlessness contrast with faith?

12. How is your lifestyle like the life of the arrogant?

How is it like the life of the righteous?

What would it mean for you to live faithfully in areas you now are not?

Study 5
Five Woes

Habakkuk 2:6-20

Purposes
☐ To discover the unifying theme of the five woes.
☐ To perceive our participation in violence and idolatry.
☐ To see the contrast between the unrighteous and God.

God's answer to Habakkuk's second complaint was begun in the early part of chapter 2. The just shall live by faith, he said, while those whose souls are not upright shall fail. In the rest of this chapter he completes his response by expanding on this theme. He gives Habakkuk a fuller picture of his view of violence.

Notes on the Text
2:6   *pledges*—"the wresting of property from their victims is compared to the taking of *pledges*. When an overlord's demand for taxes could not be met, valuables were taken from his subjects as pledges, or sureties, that the debt would be paid" (*The Broadman Bible Commentary*, Volume 8, p. 259). This might also refer to the sins of the Judeans; they were not to take interest from fellow Judeans, nor were they to inconvenience anyone by keeping some necessary item in pledge (see Ex. 22:25-27).
2:15   *drink*—the imagery here is very similar to Jeremiah 25: 15-26 where various nations (including the Chaldeans) are pictured seated around a table and each is forced to drink in turn the Lord's cup of wrath.

1. Read Habakkuk 2:6-20. This passage is structured around the various woes. How many times does the phrase *Woe to him who* appear?

Who is each addressed to?

---

2. What, in general, does God say are the consequences of doing what is warned against in each woe?

Why do you suppose people do what is warned against in these woes?

---

3. Let's look at the woes more closely. What does "gets evil gain for his house" mean (v. 9)? (Compare Jer. 22:13-14.)

What does it mean that "the stone will cry out" and "the beam from the woodwork respond" (v. 11)?

---

4. What does it mean for people to "labor only for fire" (v. 13)?

Who makes the people do this? Why?

What does verse 14 mean?

What is verse 14's connection with the rest of the third woe?

5. What is the dominant imagery of the fourth woe (vv. 15-17)?

How can the cup-of-wrath metaphor be seen as an answer to the complaint that Habakkuk expressed in his net metaphor (1:14-17)?

6. What is the primary issue in the fifth woe (vv. 18-20)?

What do we learn about the folly of idolatry, particularly through the rhetorical questions?

Why is revelation so important here?

In what ways do you fail to put your trust in the revelation of God?

7. Which of the woes do you identify most with? Why?

How are all five woes similar?

How is God, especially as seen in verses 14 and 20, contrasted with the unrighteous?

Acquisitiveness and avarice, according to Habakkuk, are essentially self-worship and lead to violence. How is this true for you personally? for the social groupings of which you are a part (national, racial, economic or religious group)?

For Further Study
1. Read Deuteronomy 32:1-43. With this context in mind, compare Deuteronomy 32:26-27 with Habakkuk 2:13-14. What do these passages teach us about who is our ultimate judge and who we ought to fear?
2. Habakkuk 2:14 appears to be a conflation of Numbers 14: 21 and Isaiah 11:9. Study the contexts of these passages. What might Habakkuk be suggesting by reiterating and combining these verses?
3. Read chapter six of Ron Sider's *Rich Christians in an Age of Hunger* (IVP). Do you think Habakkuk would agree with Sider? Why or why not?

Study 6
Habakkuk's Resolve

Habakkuk 3:1-19

Purposes
☐ To be reminded of the history of the relationship between God and his people.
☐ To understand Habakkuk's response to the way God works in history.
☐ To understand the relationship between faith and circumstances.

Theophany is a word commonly used in association with Habakkuk 3. Derived from the Greek terms for "God" and "to show," a theophany is a manifestation of the divine in the form of dreams, visions or some natural phenomenon. The Transfiguration was a theophany as were the events with Moses and the people of Israel on Mount Sinai. With the theophany of chapter 3, Habakkuk's questioning of God's character and purposes comes to rest.

Notes on the Text
3:1   *Shigionoth*—a musical instruction of uncertain meaning; therefore it is transliterated. Possibly it means this prayer is to be sung with great emotion.
3:3   *from Teman . . . from Mount Paran*—Teman, located in Edom (south of the Dead Sea), and Mount Paran, probably in a mountain range in the Sinai Peninsula, are southern regions which traditionally represent the direction from which God comes to help those in need. (See Deut. 33:2 and Judg. 5:4-5.)
3:3   *Selah*—a musical instruction commonly found in the Psalms, possibly indicating an interlude or a direc-

tion to play or sing loudly.

3:7 *Cushan . . . Midian*—probably synonymous terms for certain nomadic tribes of Edom (not to be identified with Cush, modern-day Ethiopia); again a possible reference to events described in Exodus as Israel encountered various tribes during its forty years in the desert.

3:13 *anointed*—occasionally used to refer to God's people, as in Psalms 28:8 and 105:15; more often used to refer to the king who represents the people. (See Ps. 20:6; 84:9; 89:38, 51.)

3:19 *hind*—a deer whose speed and sure-footedness were proverbial among the Hebrews.
    with stringed instruments—a musical direction given to the leader of the temple's music, indicating this prayer, and possibly the whole book, was to be used in worship.

1. What do you see as the meaning of history?

2. Read Habakkuk 3. What is the report Habakkuk heard?

In verse 2 Habakkuk says he fears the Lord's work and then goes on immediately to ask that the Lord renew it. Why?

3. What other requests does he make in verse 2?

How does this contrast with his requests of 1:2-4?

_____

_____

How can Habakkuk's approach to God in prayer be an example for you?

_____

4. The central part of Habakkuk's prayer (vv. 3-15) bears similarities to other great victory songs in Scripture like Moses' song in Exodus 15 and Deborah's song in Judges 5. None of the imagery here is so specific that it can refer to one and only one event in Israel's past. But what events from Israel's past do these verses remind you of?

_____

_____

_____

5. What does "His ways were as of old" (v. 6) say about the way God works in history?

_____

Why is this significant to Habakkuk?

_____

Consider your history with God. What aspects make you afraid (as Habakkuk was made afraid when he heard the report of what God had done, v. 2)?

_____

_____

Which aspects would you like renewed?

_____

_____

6. What purpose is stated for all of God's activity described in chapter 3?

_____

Compare 1:12 and 3:13. What do you learn?

_____

_____

7. Summarize how God is characterized in this chapter.

_____

_____

How does Habakkuk respond to God (vv. 16-19)?

_____

8. What, very likely, is the direct cause of the defoliation described in verse 17?

_____

Does Habakkuk's attitude toward this imply that God has satisfied Habakkuk's second complaint? Explain.

_____

_____

How has Habakkuk's understanding of the way God works

in history resolved his complaints against God?

9. What does this understanding of God's working in history have to do with faith?

What do circumstances have to do with faith?

How does the basis of your faith compare to the basis of Habakkuk's faith?

For Further Study
1. Compare Habakkuk 3 to the preface to the Ten Commandments (Ex. 20:2). What is significant here? Why?

Study 7
A Last Look

Habakkuk 1–3

Purposes
☐ To understand the distillation of Habakkuk found in 2:4-5.
☐ To consider more deeply how each of us participates in idolatry, violence and self-sufficiency (interpersonal *and* corporate/national).
☐ To reflect on how to live by faith.

In this final study we want to step back from Habakkuk, reflect on what we have learned, make some connections and draw some conclusions. Let this quote serve as a thought starter: "The key to the ultimate relevance and to the triumph of the good is not any calculation at all, . . . but rather simple obedience. . . . The kind of faithfulness that is willing to accept evident defeat rather than complicity with evil is, by virtue of its conformity with what happens to God when he works among men in Jesus, aligned with the triumph of the Lamb. . . . This vision of ultimate good being determined by faithfulness and not by results is the point where we modern men get off" (John Howard Yoder, *The Politics of Jesus*, p. 245).

Notes on the Text
2:4 *live by his faith*—the notion of faithfulness is included in this phrase, not just holding certain beliefs.

1. In your own words, what is God's central message to Habakkuk?

_____

_____

_____

How is 2:4 the core or distillation of Habakkuk's entire message?

_____

_____

2. In 2:4 the statement "the righteous shall live by his faith" comes as a contrast to "he whose soul is not upright in him shall fail," to the description of the "arrogant man" in 2:5 and to the five woes. Discuss the meaning of 2:4b, then, by contrasting it to the wicked and lawless as described in Habakkuk.

_____

_____

_____

How do these contrasts help you to understand what it means to be righteous and to live by faith(fulness)?

_____

_____

_____

3. How is faith related to other themes in Habakkuk (for example, waiting on God; his past and future deliverance of his people; violence, self-sufficiency and idolatry)?

_____

_____

_____

_____

4. In what ways does chapter 2 demonstrate the difference between the world's concept and God's concept of power, wealth and glory?

_____

_____

_____

5. The wickedness described in Habakkuk seems to spring from a spirit of self-sufficiency, self-importance and greed. How do these characteristics lead you to "heap up what is not your own" and to do "violence" in everyday affairs (perhaps verbal violence through gossip or put downs)?

_____

_____

_____

_____

How do these same characteristics lead to wickedness and violence in our national life (including racial, economic or social groups) and in international relations?

_____

_____

_____

What would a nation that lived by faith be like?

_____

_____

_____

6. The Christian's faith is in Jesus Christ. How is Jesus an example of the righteous living by faith?

_____

_____

_____

_____

What additional certainty of God's triumph over evil and his care for the suffering does the Christian have which Habakkuk did not have?

_____

_____

We are faced with (1) the violence of the wicked (Habakkuk's first complaint) and (2) God's righteous anger against pride, self-worship and violence of which we _all_ are guilty (God's answer). How is Jesus' death and resurrection the ultimate assurance that the righteous will *in fact* live?

_____

_____

For Further Study
1. "Grit your teeth; grin and bear it." Explain how Habakkuk's attitude in 3:17-19 differs from this type of modern stoicism.
2. Habakkuk 2:4 is quoted in Romans 1:17, Galatians 3:11 and Hebrews 10:38-39. How do these New Testament writers interpret and apply this verse from Habakkuk? Be sure to note the contexts of each passage.
3. When have you personally, your church or your country ignored the revelation God has given and taken cues from the "sure principles" of some humanly constructed idol, such as some "neutral" political ideology?
4. Look again at the quote in the introduction to this study. Do you think Habakkuk would agree with it? Why or why not? What do you think of it? Defend or criticize the assertions in the quote by reference to Habakkuk.
5. Do a comparative study of Habakkuk with Psalm 44. How are the issues and questions of the two similar? different? How are the attitudes of Habakkuk and the psalmist similar? different?

Leader's Notes

Your small group is unusual.

Few groups would commit themselves to in-depth study of an Old Testament book. Fewer still would study a prophet. And fewer yet, a minor prophet.

We feel more comfortable in the New Testament, allowing the Old Testament (by far the larger portion of the Bible) to remain wrapped in the mystery of a distant and foreign culture. Yet a full understanding of the New Testament requires an understanding of the Old.

Many of us know that Romans 1:16-17 is the kernel of Paul's most theological epistle. And we also know that these verses ("the just shall live by faith") offered Martin Luther the key to his struggles and so set the Reformation in motion. But how many of us know that Paul is making a direct quotation from the lowly prophet Habakkuk? Obviously, if we are to fully appreciate Paul, we must understand what Paul was quoting.

Nonetheless, given this general unfamiliarity with the Old Testament, you, as leader, will likely have quite a challenge on your hands: a challenge to motivate your group members and a challenge to be one step (if not two) ahead of them—that means being prepared.

By this we don't mean to imply that the leader must have at least one academic degree more than anyone else, or even that the leader must teach the rest what they do not know. Rather your task is to be a facilitator. You are to help the group members discover the truths in Habakkuk for themselves. That requires that you know your material well, not that you lecture the group. You simply have to know where to lead them.

Why? Why this discussion method of Bible study? Because there is excitement in the act of discovery. And excitement translates into motivation—motivation to study the Old Testament because you can discover its truth on your own and because God can speak to you directly. Study will lead far beyond Habakkuk to other truths of the Old Testament. While there is certainly a place for teachers in the church, there is definitely a responsibility for all of us to personally study God's Word on our own. We are all priests with one mediator, Jesus Christ.

How can you become a facilitator? *Pray*. Ask for the Spirit's illumination. God wants us to understand all of his Word, so you can confidently pray in his will. He also wants your group members to know him and his Word. Pray that God will help you be a facilitator, one who helps others grow in their own relationship with God.

Study. First move through the study yourself, noting the introductory material and the notes on the text. You might want to read through and take notes on the passage before you look at the questions in the guide, trying to understand it on your own first. A good rule of thumb is at least two hours of preparation for each study. However, you will need even more time to prepare for studies one and two.

Next, *prepare to lead*. Only after you have studied on your own should you read through the leader's notes for the study you are working on. These are intended to warn you of potential problems in group discussion and to give you hints on how to bring out the essence of the passage. It is here too that you should take a second, closer look at the purposes listed at the beginning of each study. These summarize what your group should take away with them. Now consider how each of the questions contributes toward accomplishing these goals.

You will note that each study contains some observation

questions (What does the passage say?), some interpretation questions (What does the passage mean?) and some application questions (What am I/are we going to do about this?). Don't be frustrated because the bulk are observation questions. If we are to interpret correctly, we must have a firm grasp of the content. This simply takes time and effort. Likewise, correct application requires correct interpretation. The interpretation questions might be the most interesting because they are discussion questions. Application questions might not elicit as much discussion because people can be threatened if there are faults or problems that could be mentioned. And we all fear self-exposure! Be sensitive to such feelings while helping the group make specific application to their lives. The point of Bible study, after all, is that our lives be changed because we know God better.

As you lead the study/discussion itself, you will want to keep the following in mind:

☐ Never answer your own question. If necessary, rephrase the question or ask, "Is the question clear?" Sometimes just repeating it will suffice. (The problem with answering your own questions is that discussion can be stifled if group members think the leader will do all the work for them or if they are threatened because the leader "knows so much and I don't want to show how much I don't know.")

☐ Similarly, don't be afraid of silence. Give the group time to look for answers. Remember it took you time to find the answers too.

☐ Don't be content with just one answer. Try to get several people to contribute to the discussion. Ask, "What do the rest of you think?" Even observation questions often have more than one answer.

☐ Acknowledge all contributions. Never refuse any answer. If a wrong answer comes up, ask, "Which verse led you to that conclusion?" or again, "What do the rest of you think?"

☐ Likewise, don't be afraid of controversy. It can be very stimulating. If you don't resolve an issue completely, don't be frustrated. Move on and keep it in mind for later. A subsequent study might solve the problem.

☐ Stick to the passage under consideration. Don't allow the group to hop through the Bible. Habakkuk is the context. If someone insists on cross-referencing where it is not essential, suggest a poststudy discussion of the matter. Or try asking, "Which verse in Habakkuk led you to that conclusion?"

☐ In the same way, stick to the topic under consideration. Habakkuk will stimulate many ideas. Use the purposes to help guide you on what is relevant. But again be sensitive to the needs of individuals. Don't shut them off just for the sake of keeping a rule. Still, you might be able to deal with a person more openly after the study is over.

☐ Feel free to summarize, highlight background material (such as that found in the notes on the text) or review past studies. But don't preach.

☐ Pray before, after, or before and after each study. Probably afterward would be the best time for group conversational prayer.

☐ Begin and end on time.

Many more suggestions and helps are found in James F. Nyquist's *Leading Bible Discussions* (IVP). Reading and studying through that would be well worth your time.

In all this, know that you have been prayed for. As we prepared this guide, we prayed that the truths in Habakkuk would come alive, that it would take on flesh and blood in the form of those who studied it. We were praying for you.

Study 1. A First Look: Habakkuk 1—3

Have you gone through the whole study on your own? If not, you shouldn't be here. Do it now before going on.

Finished? Okay.

This study covers a lot of ground in a short span. You'll need to have the major divisions of the book firmly in mind so you can guide the group through the study without getting bogged down on any one point.

Nevertheless, many questions could come up. Be sensitive to which can and should be answered as they arise and which should be tabled. How do you tell the difference? Look through the remaining six studies now to get an idea of what themes will be covered. With these in view you can suggest that a particular question will be answered down the road. Keep a list of questions you hope to answer in subsequent studies. Just make sure you do refer to the list and do bring up the questions later.

Of course looking through the remaining six studies at this time means you will need more time to prepare for this study than for any of the others, with the possible exception of study two.

As you worked through the first study, you probably noticed a paucity of application questions. There is good reason for this. As we said above, correct application requires correct interpretation, and correct interpretation requires correct observation. As the studies progress, more and more application questions are introduced.

One way to summarize this study at the close would be to have two group members do a dramatic reading of the entire book, one taking Habakkuk's part and the other, God's. Encourage your two volunteers not just to read but to infuse their readings with the obvious emotion both Habakkuk and God express. The group's responses to questions 8 and 9 should give good clues to this. Such a reading could help make the whole book more understandable to everyone.

Question 1. This question might not elicit much response. Admittedly it is very broad. The intent is to leave open many avenues of response. If the group has trouble, you might be prepared to spark discussion with specific examples of injustice from the newspaper or "60 Minutes." Try to focus on noncontroversial examples, that is, examples that all would agree represent injustice. The idea is not to discuss whether this or that incident is or is not unjust, rather it is to focus on how you respond when you see injustice.

Question 2. We suggest reading the book aloud. The first question should help you answer the second.

Question 5. Dialog involves more than just the fact that two

people are talking. Listening, changing, responding to what
is said rather than with a formula are all examples of what else
is involved. Look for these and others in the dialog between
Habakkuk and God.

Before you break, be sure you remind the group to read
and study 2 Chronicles 33—36 and, if possible, to work
through study two before your next meeting. There is even
more material to cover here than in study one. It will be
virtually impossible to do an adequate study unless everyone
is prepared.

Study 2. Habakkuk in Perspective: 2 Chronicles 33—36

This could well be the most difficult study in this guide. Once
again, as leader you need to be very familiar with the passage so you can prevent discussion from getting bogged
down. This will certainly mean reading the passage over
several times and carefully studying the maps, the time chart
and the notes on the text. Perhaps the following summary of
the historical events before and during the time of 2 Chronicles 33—36 will also help.

The fortunes of Israel worsened steadily after Solomon,
though for a brief period under Jeroboam II (782-753 B.C.)
the kingdom flourished again. From the time of Tiglath-
pileser (identified as Pul in 2 Kings 15:19) of Assyria (745-727
B.C.), Judah was strapped with heavy duties by Assyria to
the point of impoverishment. This continued until the decay
of the Assyrian Empire in the last quarter of the seventh century B.C. (ca. 625 B.C.). Josiah's reformation hints at the
Assyrians' loss of authority in Palestine.

The fall of Ninevah in 612 B.C. was the death blow to the
Assyrian Empire, but more battles remained. Into the power
vacuum in Palestine stepped Pharaoh Neco in the final years
of the seventh century B.C. Neco was on his way to Carchemish in 609 B.C. to join the waning Assyrian Empire in
opposing the rising Babylonia (Chaldean) power led by
Nebuchadnezzar when Josiah intercepted him at Megiddo
(2 Chron. 35:22; and see map). The battle of Carchemish was

won by Nebuchadnezzar in 605 B.C. Egypt retained power in Palestine for a time, but (as seen in 2 Chron. 36:4)6) this situation soon changed. Nebuchadnezzar and the Chaldeans took control.

Since Habakkuk speaks of the rise of the Chaldeans (after 612 and 605 B.C. they were clearly the dominant power in the Middle East) but does not mention the siege of Jerusalem (587 B.C.) except as a future event, the book is reasonably dated between 612 and 587 B.C., and more probably during the reign of Jehoiakim (609-597 B.C.). This is supported by the fact that the moral conditions described by Habakkuk match those of Judah during Jehoiakim's reign.

If not everyone read 2 Chronicles 33—36 before the study, give time to scan the passage. It is too long to read aloud.

Question 3. Don't let the last part be answered only by considering Manasseh. It is fine if he needs to be considered first to help the group understand the broader question, "For what purpose does God use the nations?" But make sure the broader question is considered as well.

Question 4. Several things are going on here. You might want to highlight these for the group through questions or brief comments. Obviously neither the people nor the king remembered God's covenant promises. And even if they did, they did not see or chose not to see the close tie between their religious and social faithfulness and their international relations.

Study 3. The Dialog Begins: Habakkuk 1:1-11
Finally you are able to turn your attention to a bite-sized chunk of Scripture. Chew it well and savor it. Some of the issues raised here will recur throughout the book, especially those of faith, violence, idolatry and how these are seen today. You might jot a few brief notes after the study is over on what different group members said. It could be interesting to look at later, perhaps in study seven, to see if any changes in perspective have come from a deeper study of Habakkuk.

Study 4. The Dialog Continues: Habakkuk 1:12—2:5

The remaining major questions and issues of the book are introduced in this passage. Their resolution is the focus of the rest of Habakkuk. So be patient and encourage the group to be patient if you are frustrated with the answers you come up with. The intent here is to get a clear grasp of the problems. The answers are developed more clearly later.

Question 1. Take several minutes on this question. Let several members contribute. Draw out their understanding of a just judge by using follow-up questions: Why is that characteristic you mention so important? Could a judge be just without being compassionate? without being objective? without having all the facts? The point is, of course, to help sensitize the members to what justice is (a concept most of us think we understand but which can be elusive and difficult to define). Help them identify with Habakkuk too. He understood God to have a character incompatible with the way he was working through the Chaldeans.

Question 2. One aspect of the last question here is Habakkuk's reviewing of the facts, the things he is certain of—a wise strategy when confusion arises in our relation to God and the faithful life.

Question 4. Why God seems to make people like fish about to be caught is not answered here. If the discussion gets hung up, make a note and suggest that the question may be answered further on. As it turns out, question 5 of the next study might give some clues. The second part of this question usually draws the answer *God* from some discussion members. Besides noting the grammatical change from second person *thou* to third person *he*, you should also encourage group members to consider the similarity of verses 15-17 to verses 5-11. *He* most likely refers to the Chaldean king as the key representative of his nation.

Question 10. Further studies, especially studies 6 and 7, pursue the topic of faith at greater depth. Don't look for airtight, theologically perfect definitions. Just get some basic facts out in the open as a departure point for later discussion.

Study 5. Five Woes: Habakkuk 2:6-20
This study provides you with an opportunity for in-depth discussion of the various evils already alluded to in Habakkuk. God's perspective on unrighteousness becomes abundantly clear. It is important to help the group understand the dynamics of evil so they can see it more clearly in their own lives and in the world. The main purpose of the study, then, is to see how the various evils are unified in a few central ideas. If your group succeeds only in making a shopping list of evils, you will have failed. The questions are, rather, What is evil? and, Why commit evil acts at all? This of course requires looking at the individual items on the list. But go beyond them to your primary objective.
Question 1. The last question here ("Who is each [woe] addressed to?") is essentially asking for a brief summary of each woe.
Question 3. The last question here will invite follow-up questions such as, Why will the stone cry out? What is it saying?
Question 4. It would probably help you to look at the first question in the For Further Study section. With this under your belt, you will be better prepared to handle questions that arise over 2:13-14.
Question 5. The note on the text for 2:15 should prove instructive if the group has difficulty with these questions.

Study 6. Habakkuk's Resolve: Habakkuk 3:1-19
Occasionally in the Old Testament, particular psalms occur in books other than the book of Psalms. Eventually they were included in the psalter. For example, part of David's prayer of thanksgiving in 1 Chronicles 16:8-36 was later included as the ninety-sixth psalm. Habakkuk contains a psalm which was not later included in the psalter itself. Its form (Shiggion, see Ps. 7; note too the closing of 3:19 which is a liturgical note found in fifty-five other psalms), the use of *selah* and the existence of some formal characteristics of Hebrew poetry (such as parallelism, note 3:5) all make it clear that this is indeed a

psalm in the formal sense. Reading the article on poetry in *The New Bible Dictionary* or the introduction to Derek Kidner's commentary *Psalms 1–72* should give you some help in understanding the chapter.

Question 1. The purpose of this question is to set the tone, not merely to define the word *history*. Although you won't come up with a complete or final answer, help the members probe the significance of human events. You might also ask such questions as, Is history significant at all? Explain. What is the meaning of life? What is the meaning of your history? (Don't take more than ten minutes.)

Question 2. Answer these questions by keeping Habakkuk 1—2 in mind.

Question 4. Verse 5 might remind some group members of the plagues God inflicted on Egypt before the Pharaoh allowed Israel to go; verse 10 might remind some of Israel's crossing of the Red Sea or the Jordan River; verse 11 might remind others of the incident recorded in Joshua 10:12-14.

Question 8. If the group has trouble answering the first question here, refer them back to 1:5-17.

Study 7. A Last Look: Habakkuk 1—3

This study provides an opportunity to reflect on what people have learned from Habakkuk over the past six weeks. If it seems more like a bull session than the other studies, do not worry. The discussion will not necessarily be any less founded on the text; people will be drawing conclusions from what they have learned so far and will be giving more attention to application of Habakkuk's message. While keeping this in mind, you must nevertheless, keep the group moving through the questions.

You may wish to have in mind one of the questions from the For Further Study section to add to this study if there is time. For example, to question 6 in the study proper you could add question 2 from For Further Study. Or to question 5 you could add question 3 from the supplementary questions. In any case, you will need to be sensitive to the time and the interests of the group.

Question 5. If the group gets hung up on the last question (on the fact that their country is not God's "new Israel"), remind them that God's Word to Habakkuk came as a prediction of judgment on the Chaldeans (a pagan nation, not God's chosen people) as well as on Judah. You might also note that Nahum is a prophecy against Assyria; Obadiah is about Edom (Israel's pagan half brother).